Preface

At thirty-three, I finally became a
daddy. I was about as prepared for
this as a kindergartner going for
their SAT. No book could ever
prepare me for the roller coaster I
was about to go on. My life as I
knew it was about to change forever.

My social life ceased to exist, my wife went through changes that occur in exorcisms, my Mustang turned in to a Suburban and I found my hair growing grey faster than a tween can upload a selfie.

Now, do not let this scare you. No no no! This is supposed to be the most exciting experience of your life, bro! You have done the only thing you were purposefully put on this earth to accomplish. You had only one solemn task and you finally did it. Who said you would never accomplish anything in life?

This is by no means a self-help book. These are simply observations of an overwhelmed and overly sarcastic stay at home dad. Do not take it literally. I will not be held

responsible for any injuries to
yourself or others while you are
using this book.

Dedication

This book is dedicated to my wife, Sara. Her hard work, dedication and integrity have been nothing but infectious catalysts to an otherwise underachieving and self-centered husband. Without her, none of this would be possible. Literally.

To my children Kaylen, Bella and Abigail; may the road rise up to meet you and may the stars always shine in your favor. This world is a beautiful place. It is the biggest gift you will ever be given and should be treated as nothing less. Never put up with anything less than what you deserve.

Babies are amazingly beautiful
stinky little creatures which after
they are born, there is no escaping
them.

Mommy might say that you do not need to go to the appointments, but this is a trap.... A bamboo pit trap.

Daddy rarely gets the "hot" shower.

Daddy rarely gets a shower period.

Baby food is just daddy food thrown
in a blender until it becomes a
milkshake. A gross, salt and pepper-
less milkshake. Delicious!

You should never try to adapt the "clean as you go" concept to the feeding process. Of all the scientists at NASA, not one of those dudes could have published something on this and saved me the time.

You are never right as a dad. Ever. Especially in a house full of girls. In no way, shape, situation or form are you right. This should be chapter one in all baby books. Even the ones for moms.

Do not try to do anything with your
baby's hair except part it with a
brush and leave it. Even this is
trekking in dark territory. Save
mommy the time of undoing that
"Flock of Seagulls" look you think is
so funny.

As daddies, we do not make rules anymore. Anywhere. If by chance you slip up and make a rule, it will be ignored. Your children make the rules now. For a few years anyways

The dog will only need attention
right this second when daddy has one
baby crying, one baby with poo up
their back and a toddler hanging out
in the neighbor's bird bath naked.

Baby walkers were not designed for us. Nor were they designed for the off-road-like conditions the stairs offer.

A baby's first words are usually
daddy or dada as it is easier to
articulate than mommy or mama.
Amazing, right?! Just remember that
for about the next month, "daddy" or
"dada" is the only word that baby
knows.

You will realize you have control
over nothing. Except the thermostat.
That is all you have that is yours.
Protect it.

You are going to find that the

commercial on tv with the crying

baby will wake you out of the

deepest sleep for no reason. That

kind of dark advertising should be

banned.

Watching your baby wake up is like watching the most beautiful sunrise.

Formula costs $21.33 per pound.

Uranium costs $20.25 a pound. Use

that at your next trivia night out in 8

years.

There is something to be said about

the analogy between laundry and

"The Song That Never Ends".

That three point five seconds
between when the old diaper comes
off and the new diaper goes on will
be as close to gambling as you are
going to come for quite some time.

The amount of money you spend on
diapers will be the reason your kid is
paying for their own college.

The only thing that drools as much as a teething baby is a St. Bernard.

Played football back in the day, huh?

New game! Follow everyone around

and turn off lights. The difference?

You probably won a few football

games.

Nothing will make a baby poo faster

than the feeling of a fresh diaper on

their hind end. This will always

happen after bath time.

Babies will sleep through anything when until about 6 months. I am talking dogs barking at the postman, mowers, apocalyptic wars... Until you close your eyes. Babies can hear that from three rooms away.

Strollers were only ever tested on short people. That shin high bar would offer the same support just three inches higher.

No matter how long ago a baby has
eaten, there is always potential for
them to throw up in your mouth
during a round of airplane.

Having twins, a trip to the grocery store means one cart is used strictly as a personnel carrier. Another cart must be obtained for rations.

Trying to put a onesie on a 4-month-old is what I imagine fighting Conor McGregor is like.

"Patty Cake" is actually "Pat A Cake". I was thirty-three when I found out.

The dudes with the Jeep wave have

nothing on the dad with a stroller

nod.

Bibs are just backwards capes.

Best time to start brushing up on dad

jokes? As soon as that pregnancy

test hits the garbage can.

Never assume you will sleep in
unless you have a written permission
slip from mommy.

Never assume you will sleep in

unless you have a written permission

slip from the babies.

Two words: Lysol. Nothing will test

your constitution like a sick baby.

Especially at three AM.

When it comes to cleaning the house, just assume your job will not be good enough. Daddy just cannot clean the same ways mommies can. They have a sixth sense about this stuff. That hair ball you missed behind the television stand? She will find it like a bloodhound.

Corned beef and cabbage is not the

best idea for a "transition" food.

You will never have bought more
batteries in your life. I am positive
that the amount of batteries I have
bought at Costco have put a
shareholder's kid through college.

Accept certain inalienable truths. You will stumble. You will not be perfect. The babies are going to get hurt, they are going to eat things they are not supposed to, they are going to smash their fingers in cabinets, and they are going to cry for no reason at all. This will be the most trying and difficult time of your life and there is no end. Even when they are long gone from your home and moved on with life you are still going to worry about them.

But then there are the smiles, the laughs, the first words, the first crawl, the first step, first Christmas, the feeling the first time they wrap their little arms around your neck. You are going to cry. You are going to cry a lot. Babies can take the biggest strongest man and turn them into the gentlest giant. Embrace it

and hold on. Before you know it,

they will be walking right out the

door.

Made in the USA
Monee, IL
17 April 2022

94889447R00028